THE
Fabulous World
THAT
God Made

By JOYCE K. ELLIS • Illustrated by ANDRÉS F. LANDAZÁBAL

beaming
books

MINNEAPOLIS

25 24 23 22 21 20 19   1 2 3 4 5 6 7 8 9

Hardcover ISBN: 9781506448572

Written by Joyce K. Ellis
Illustrated by Andrés F. Landazábal
Designed by Sarah DeYoung, Mighty Media
Production by Lauren Williamson, 1517 Media

Library of Congress Cataloging-in-Publication Data

Names: Ellis, Joyce K., author. | Landazábal, Andrés, illustrator.
Title: The fabulous world that God made / written by Joyce K. Ellis ;
   illustrated by Andrés Landazábal.
Description: Minneapolis, MN : Beaming Books, 2019. | Summary: God forms the
   sun, land, water, animals, and the first people in this creation story.
Identifiers: LCCN 2018030447 | ISBN 9781506448572 (hard cover : alk. paper)
Subjects: | CYAC: Creation--Fiction. | God--Fiction.
Classification: LCC PZ7.E4735 Fab 2019 | DDC [E]--dc23 LC record available at https://lccn.loc.
gov/2018030447

VN0004589; 9781506448572; JAN2019

Beaming Books
510 Marquette Avenue
Minneapolis, MN 55402
Beamingbooks.com

A NOTE FROM THE AUTHOR

The Fabulous World That God Made brings the creation story to life for kids, using the classic rhythm, repetition, humor, and cumulative storytelling style of "This Is the House That Jack Built." As you look at the illustrations with young children, you can point out the animals and other gifts God created for us. Ask older children to identify and point them out to you as you read. Children delight in taking part in the storytelling, so as they get used to the repetition, pause before the phrase "in the fabulous world that God made" and let them fill in the blank—or say it with them. Try this technique with other phrases as well. The children may pick up on this and do it on their own.

Whenever you go for a walk, visit a zoo, or enjoy the wonder of an aquarium, take the opportunity to point out God's amazing handiwork in all he created. The biblical account of God's loving act of creation shapes our understanding of God and plants the seeds of faith in our hearts.

Most importantly, this retelling of God's creation emphasizes that he made human beings special, breathing into them his own breath. Talk with your children about how precious each of us is to God. He wants a personal relationship with each of us. God has plans for each of us. And he wants each of us to be like him, to love him, and to serve him always.

—Joyce K. Ellis

This is the darkness that filled all of space
before
the fabulous world that God made.

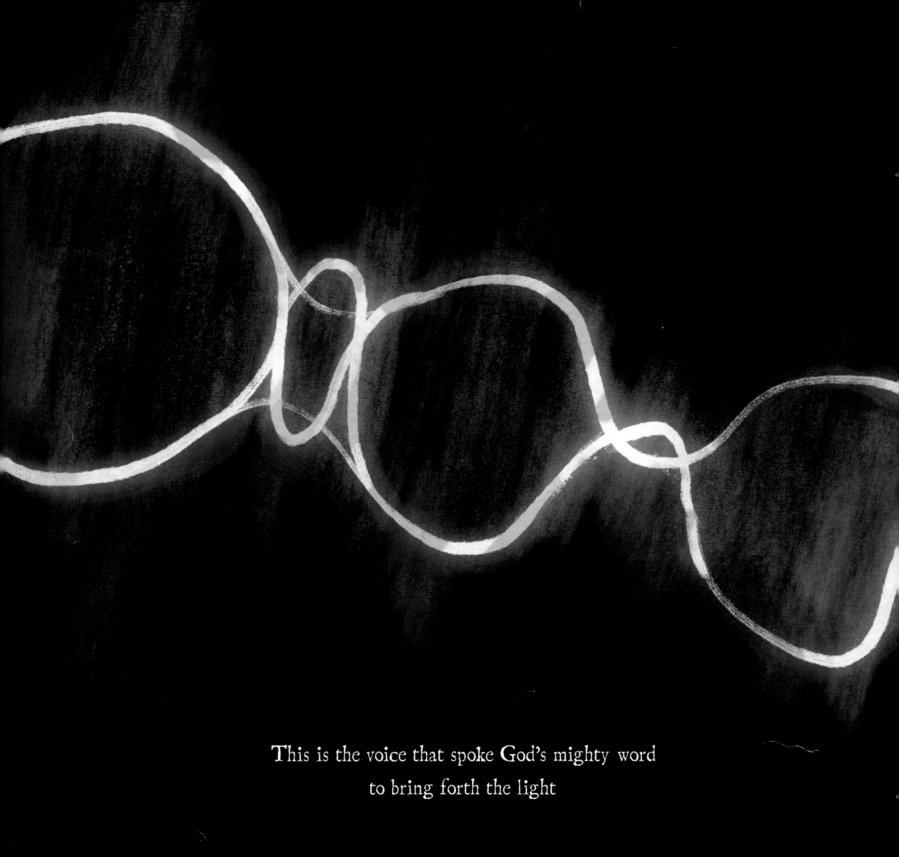

This is the voice that spoke God's mighty word
to bring forth the light

in the darkness that ruled
and filled all of space
in the fabulous world that God made.

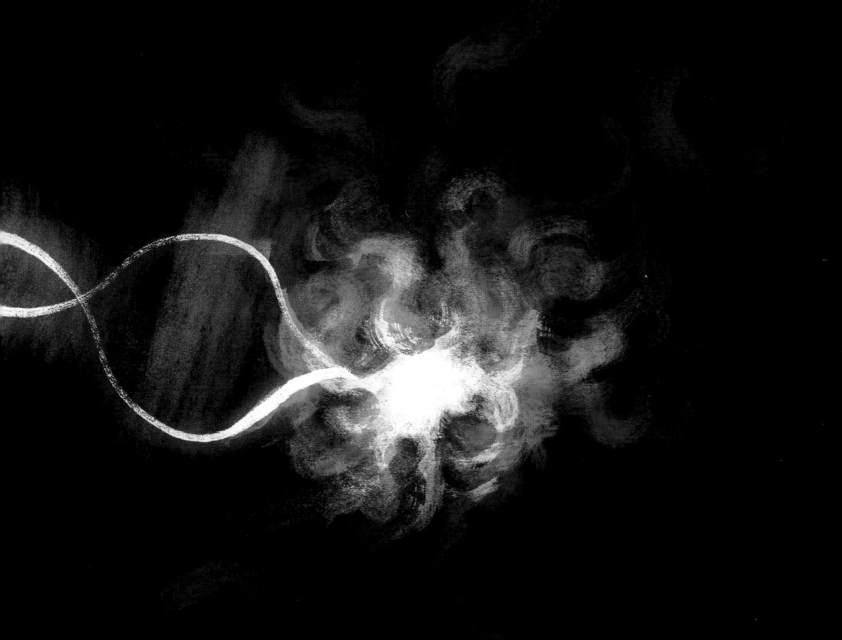

This is the sun that God hung way up high
to light up the day,

then he welcomed the moon
to light up the night
and shatter the darkness
that filled all of space
in the fabulous world that God made.

These are the hands that reached out in great love
and divided the heavens from earth down below
in the bright, shimmering light
that shattered the darkness
that filled all of space
in the fabulous world that God made.

These are the lands and the oceans God shaped
and put under the heavens

in the bright, shimmering light
that shattered the darkness
that filled all of space
in the fabulous world that God made.

These are the grasses, the tulips, and oaks
God planted on earth
and put under the heavens

in the bright, shimmering light
that shattered the darkness
that filled all of space
in the fabulous world that God made.

These are the dolphins, the penguins and whales,
the great sharks and otters,
the clown fish and seals
that swam free in the seas
that God parted from land
in the fabulous world that God made.

These are the parrots, the cardinals and geese,
the herons and toucans,
the bats and the bees

that flew high in the skies
up above land and seas
in the fabulous world that God made.

These are the horses, the cheetahs and frogs,
the snakes and giraffes, and the monkeys and dogs
that trotted and swung,
hopped and slithered and ran,
and ate from the grasses and flowers and trees

that covered the land
in the bright, shimmering light
that shattered the darkness
that filled all of space
in the fabulous world that God made.

These are the humans that God set apart
like no other creatures he'd made until then:
two people created in God's special plan
to be like him and love him and serve him each day.

God shaped the first man from the dust of the ground,
and he breathed out his breath to bring Adam to life.

Then God made a woman for Adam, named Eve,
a side-by-side-partner
to love and be loved.

This woman and man, in their own special ways,
looked after the hippos, the zebras and bears,
the lilies and violets, the palm trees and pines
that grew strong on the land

in the bright, shimmering light
that shattered the darkness
that filled all of space
in the fabulous world that God made.

So...
look all around
at the land and the seas,
the animals, stars, and the plants, and the trees.

And look at the people, like you and like me, that God has some plans for,
like Adam and Eve.
God calls us, together, to care for these gifts,
to be like him and love him and serve him each day

in the **fan-TAB-u-lous** world that God made!

ABOUT THE AUTHOR

JOYCE K. ELLIS has been writing, editing, and teaching for more than forty years. She has published hundreds of articles and more than a dozen fiction and nonfiction books, including the Gold Medallion Award–winning *One-Minute Bible for Kids*. She and her husband have three grown children and seven grandchildren. Joyce enjoys traveling, a good cup of tea, and reading beside a lake, river, or ocean.

ABOUT THE ILLUSTRATOR

ANDRÉS F. LANDAZÁBAL is an illustrator and art director based in Armenia, Colombia. His work has appeared in film, television, and print for companies such as Sesame Street, Discovery Kids, and Fox. Andrés's love for drawing and painting was instilled at a young age through the reading of classic illustrated children's books.